PUT IT SIMPLY

The Easy Option to Earn Income and Reduce Cost Basis

Part One

> "Everything should be made as simple as possible, but no simpler."
>
> -Albert Einstein

My goal is to present my favorite options strategy to both novice and advanced traders by teaching you just the essential principles and caveats before discussing the more advanced tweaks and technicalities.

In my years as a student suffering through college and law school lectures, bad professors seemed to be the norm rather than the exception. These professors were more concerned about showing us how much they knew about a subject, while caring less about whether we actually learned anything useful. I will not do that in this Book. I will explain the strategy in the simplest manner, by focusing on only the crucial 20%. The remaining 80% consists of technicalities (e.g., "the Greeks") and strategy tweaks that you should definitely learn, but not until you understand the crucial 20%. College syllabi often follow an opposite approach, leaving students in a state of confusion throughout the semester as their oblivious professors pile proverbial bricks atop foundations that were never fully formed.

For the advanced options traders reading this, here is the TL/DR ("Too Long/Didn't Read") abbreviated summary of the strategy in two sentences. Do **not** read the abbreviated summary that follows if you don't already understand options, as this will confuse and intimidate you. Instead, wait until I explain these terms and concepts over the next few pages, and then come back to refresh your understanding. And if you are an experienced options trader who is already familiar with naked puts and credit spreads and believes they are too risky or not profitable, please give the remaining pages at least a cursory glance to see if they can change your opinion.

The Concise "BLUF" Summary (For Advanced Options Traders Only)

If you already thoroughly understand options, here is a **Bottom-Line Up-Front (BLUF)** quick explanation of the primary strategy:

DON'T READ THIS UNLESS YOU ALREADY KNOW WHAT A SHORT PUT IS

1) Select a stock you would like to own, for which you have the cash/margin to purchase 100 shares.

2) Wait for a day on which the stock is trading significantly down and IV (implied volatility) is peaking.

3) Select an OTM put **delta** based on the price at which you would like to own 100 shares (I recommend going no farther than a -.20 put delta).

4) Select an expiration date (I recommend between a week to a month out).

5) Put in a slightly optimistic GTC limit-sell order at the upper end of the bid/ask spread. If you are selling multiple contracts, use progressively higher laddered-limit orders for each contract.

Put it Simply

Quick (and Mandatory) Disclaimer:

Though this strategy is one of the safest options strategies you can employ. All investing carries risk. I am unaware of any completely "risk free" investment. Don't follow my advice if you are unable to accept any financial risk.

For Novices: A Simplified Summary Of The Concept

Okay, now that you have bypassed the intimidating preceding paragraph intended for advanced traders only, here is the thousand-foot view of the concept in plain speak.

There are two reasons why this strategy has provided me with more consistently profitable returns than <u>all</u> the other strategies I have tested since 2012.

Reason #1: Even if you "lose" by implementing this strategy, you are still rewarded, at a lower cost, with the long stock that you were ready and willing to own.

Reason #2: When you win at this strategy, you keep the premium and can rinse and repeat it as often as you'd like.

Let's say you are bullish on Tesla (TSLA) and TSLA is trading at $600. Because you are bullish on TSLA, you would like to own the shares now, and would even be willing to buy them at a cost basis of $600. But wouldn't it be better if you could give yourself a month to lock in a purchase price of $550 or even $500 per share instead?

Now, if you are familiar with call options, you could purchase a $500 call on TSLA and give yourself the right to purchase the shares at a price lower than where TSLA is currently trading, but there are several problems with this strategy. First, when you buy a call, you are immediately spending money, and if the call is for a price lower than the current trading price, this is an "In-the-Money" call, and can be <u>very</u> expensive. And for every trading day where the stock remains steady or goes down, your call will normally lose money. At the end of the expiration, if the call that you purchased is higher than the trading price of the underlying shares (e.g.,$550 TSLA call when TSLA is trading at $500) then there would be no reason to exercise your right to purchase the shares at a price higher than what you could purchase them for on the market. Your call option would have "expired worthless" and you will lose 100% of the money you spent on the call.

So Why Not Spend The Money To Buy A Call?

Buying call options is how many options traders make the transition from long stocks to options. The reason for this is that buying a call option is always cheaper than buying 100 shares of the underlying stock (the "underlying") at market value. And since one call option gives you the "right, but not the obligation" to purchase the shares ("control the shares") at a price lower than where you think they will be trading at the end of the expiration period, a call option is a leveraged, defined-risk, strategy. It is leveraged because you are spending a little to control a lot, and it is defined-risk because you know exactly how much money you are risking in buying a call option, which is the amount you spent to purchase the call option. When buying options, the most you can lose is the amount you spent to purchase the option.

Many traders are attracted to the low cost of entry when buying out of the money options because it seems like "it can't hurt." The problem is that it can. When you buy an out-of-the-money (OTM) option, you must be correct on three fronts in order to be profitable.

First. You must be correct about the direction. When you buy an OTM call, you are buying a call at a strike price higher than the market price of the underlying asset, believing that the stock will continue to rise past the strike price. The higher the strike price is above the market price, the lower the premium. If the market price advances past the strike price, the buyer of the option benefits from the capital appreciation, almost as if he had bought the shares long in the open market. If that doesn't happen, and instead the stock price falls below the strike price, the buyer won't want to exercise the option and will have forfeited the premium he paid for it.

The buyer also must take into account the implied volatility (IV) of the stock. The higher the IV, the greater the possibility of a large move - either up or down. Therefore, the more volatile the stock, the more valuable the option. To see this in action, look at a stock chart with the implied volatility technical indicator overlaid. Now bring up a few random stocks around their recent earnings dates. Notice how the IV almost (but not always) rises 1) before earnings and 2) on days when the stock price is falling. So think of the cost of IV as a risk premium. Spiking IV is good for the option seller and bad for the option buyer.

Second. The buyer also must select a realistic OTM strike price. The farther away that the strike price is from the price at which the stock is currently trading, the lower the likelihood (in direct proportion) the stock will rise to hit the OTM strike price.

Third. The buyer has to consider the option's time to expiration since an option with a longer expiration period has a greater probability of moving in the desired direction and would therefore have greater value to the buyer. An option buyer will still lose all of the money he paid for an option if he was correct about the direction, and the strike price, but wrong about the time it took the stock to arrive at the strike price.

So, you still think buying calls are the way to go? In case it's not obvious, a cheap, out-of-the-money call is not much different from buying a lottery ticket. The odds of success are generally not in your favor, as several studies have shown that most options expire worthless.

When you buy out-of-the-money options, whether a call or a put, you will have a low probability of a high profitability. In other words, the outcome will be highly profitable compared to the money invested, but only if you are right.

How to Understand This Strategy Through the Context of A Fire Insurance Policy

Let's say you are selling somebody a fire insurance policy on his home. The home is currently worth $500K. You like this home and would be happy to own it for $500K because the property value looks likely to appreciate in the future. However, if you could buy the property for less than $500K, you would be thrilled. The homeowner says he would not want to own the home if the value drops below $300K. So, in exchange for your promise to buy the home from the homeowner if its value drops below $300K, the homeowner will pay you a recurring monthly payment ("premium") of $100. Each month there is no negative event that affects the value of the house, you pocket the $100. Five years and $6000 in collected premiums later, there is a garage fire. The rest of the house is fine, but the appraised value of the house is now $400K due to the smoke damage. Since you and the homeowner are now aware of the heightened risk, you both renegotiate the terms of the policy. The homeowner will now pay you $150 per month and you promise to buy the house if its value falls to $250K. Now, after five more years, and $9000 in collected premiums, the homeowner inadvertently burns down his house. The appraised value of the property lot is $240K. If (and only if) the homeowner wishes to exercise his right and assign you the obligation to purchase his home, will you then be obligated to purchase his home for the pre-negotiated price ("strike price") of $250K. You are pleased. This is a home that you did want to own. You were ready to purchase it for $500K, but decided to hold out for a better deal. Because you waited, you were finally able to purchase the home for $250K. And as consideration for waiting, you were compensated $15,000 in total premiums over 10 years.

I know that some of you skeptics will protest: "You just paid $250K for a home that is only worth $240K!" Here is why that is not a problem: First of all, you could have paid full price ($500K) for the home 10 years ago. There was no guarantee that the home was going to appreciate, just an optimistic assumption. If you had paid that full amount then, and the home suffered the same two fires, you would be looking at a 50% loss in its value now. Furthermore, you would have also paid out $15,000 in premiums over that period for the fire insurance, resulting in a house with an actual value of $235,000.

Let's bring the fire-insurance analogy back to our put selling strategy. You gave yourself a potential opportunity to purchase something you wanted to own (equity shares), at a strike price lower than their value at the time of the contract (out of the money put), while you made a nice monthly profit (premium).

And keep in mind that the total premiums are generally far larger than any dividend you would have received during the same timeframe.

What's the Catch to This Strategy?

It goes without saying, but in case it doesn't: all investments carry risks. Even keeping your money in bonds carries risks. So here are the risks you need to be aware of with this strategy.

Risk #1 - Missed Capital Appreciation: When you postpone purchasing shares for an equity that you're bullish on, you stand to miss out on the huge gains it might make during the expiration period. This is because you won't be owning the shares *until the price drops low enough for them to be "put" to you* through an options assignment, should the price fall to the strike price you had mutually agreed to.

Risk #2 - Missed Dividend: Also while you wait, you will forego any dividends that the stock pays to the record holders prior to the stock's ex-dividend date, since you don't currently own the shares.

Risk #3 - Having to Purchase For Below Market Value: If you view this as an unacceptable risk, then you shouldn't utilize this strategy. Remember that if you had gone out and purchased the shares instead of selling the put, then you would be left with shares you had purchased at full price which are now worth less if the stock price plummets. This is not a bad thing if you intended to sell the put with the desire to own the stock. You avoided the capital loss that the previous owner suffered and are now buying the stock at a discount. This is similar to buying a brand new car versus waiting for two years to buy that same car. Somebody is going to suffer the capital loss; it's preferable for that person to not be you, so you can swoop in and purchase that car for a discount.

Explanation Of How This Strategy Works

Step 1. First, decide which stock you are bullish on and would like to own. As I will discuss in an upcoming book, I have found it significantly more effective to maintain and monitor a smaller group of stocks compared to a larger group. Each stock has its own trading signature, such as how they tend to respond to overbought/oversold technical indicators. If you know from experience that TSLA usually rebounds when it goes severely oversold, you can profit from this knowledge and experience because you will have the confidence to sell a put when TSLA is tanking and put and IV premiums are spiking, as less familiar traders seek to exit their positions because they aren't familiar with this typical trading signature of TSLA.

It is difficult to become intimately familiar with the signature of one stock, let alone many, so give yourself time to carefully follow one stock before adding more to your portfolio.

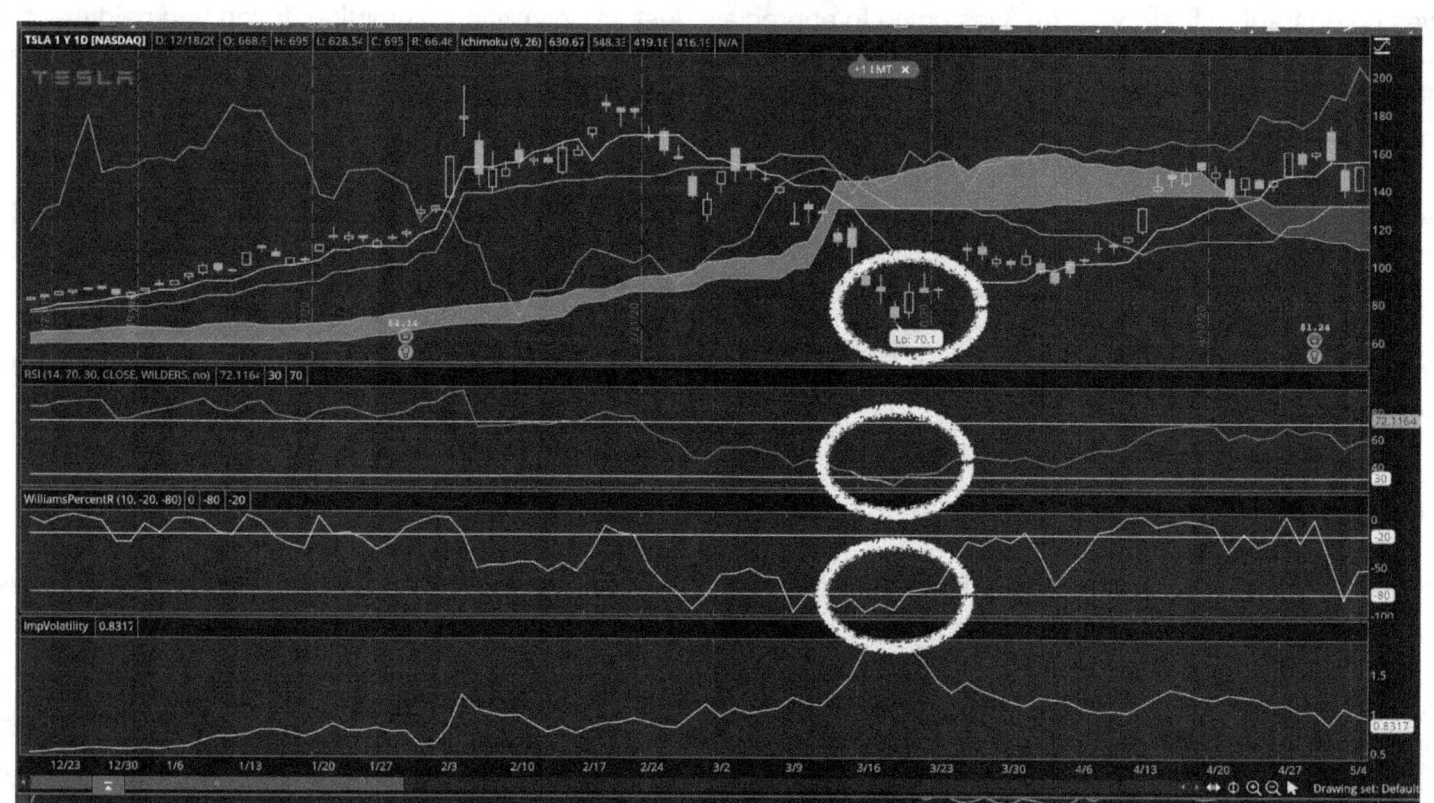

When the RSI and WilliamsPercentR both go below the oversold line at the same time, I have found that TSLA tends to sharply recover.

Step 2. Next, decide at what price you would ideally like to own this stock. Let's continue with the TSLA example. If you would like to own TSLA now, you could sell an at-the-money put, in which its strike price is the closest strike to its current market price. So if TSLA is currently selling at $603, you would sell the $600 put. If you sold the $605 put, that would be an in-the-money put. Although the premium you would collect would be even richer than the at-the-money put, you face an increased possibility of early assignment, which means you could be assigned the shares early, at a price higher than its market value, before expiration. I normally sell my puts between the .10 and .20 (absolute value) put delta. Although both put deltas are measured in the negative, I am using absolute value for the deltas here for simplicity. Just know that a .20 put (technically a -.20 put) normally carries somewhere around an 80% possibility of closing out-of-the-money at expiration. A .10 put is even farther

Put it Simply

away from the money and carries around a 90% possibility of closing out-of-the-money at expiration. The farther away from the current strike price, the less premium you will take in, the lower the probability you will end up being assigned the shares, and the lower the cost basis for the shares if you do get assigned.

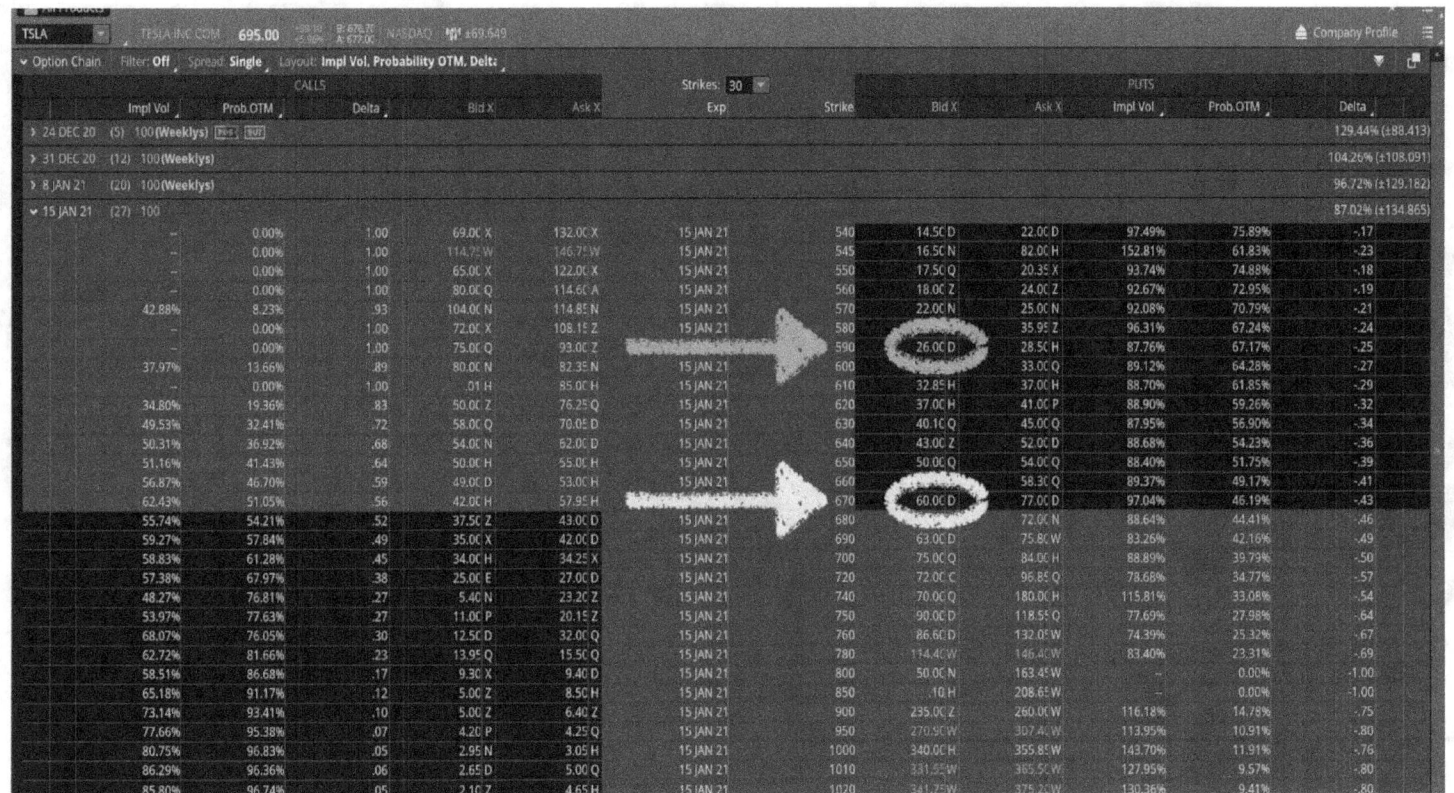

The blue arrow and oval shows that if you sold the 15JAN2021 $590 strike on TSLA, you could expect to take in a premium of about $2,600. The yellow shows that if you sold the $670 strike, you could expect to take in a premium of about $6000. These figures are based on 27 days to expiration.

Step 3. Lastly, decide on an expiration for the put you are selling. The further out you sell, the greater the opportunity for the stock to fall towards the strike price, and the greater the premium you will take in. You may find that if you were to sell a -.10 delta[1] put with a monthly expiration, you can get about the same premium as if you were to sell a -.40 delta put with a weekly expiration. Always keep track of when earnings are, as stocks tend to make large moves immediately following quarterly earnings and you don't want to be caught off-guard. One way around earnings surprises is to not sell stocks that announce earnings and to opt for index funds instead, such as the SPY Exchange Traded Fund (ETF). But if you have strong reason to believe, based on your backtesting, that a certain stock rarely falls below a certain put delta, such as the -.10 put delta, then you might be able to maximize your profits by selling a -.10 put delta immediately before earnings. This is because IV often tends to peak in the pre-earnings uncertainty, and collapse after the quarterly earnings are announced and the uncertainty resolves itself.

---

[1] Although the minus sign may be occasionally omitted, for the purposes of this book, assume that all references to short put deltas shall be negative deltas.

Put it Simply

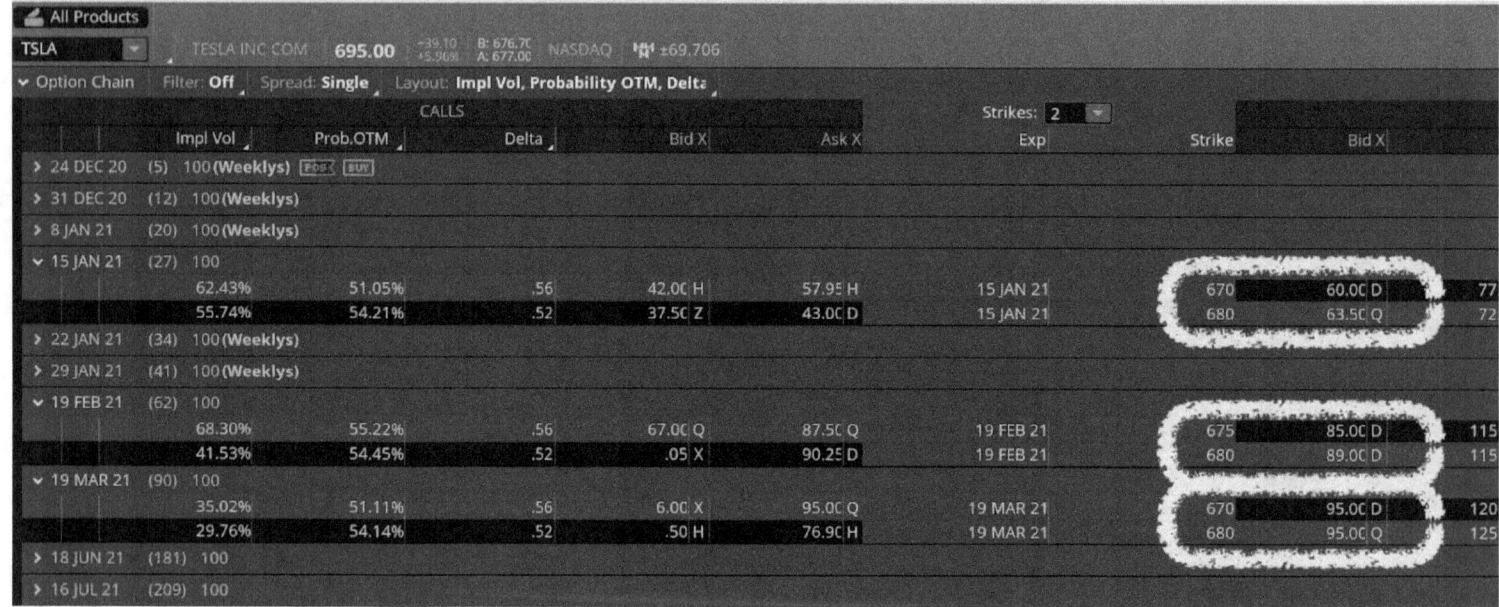

Notice the increases in premium for similar strikes for each month. Selling the $670 strike about a month from the time this screenshot was taken would yield about $6000 in premium, whereas selling the 19 March 2021 $670 strike would yield about $9,500.

What Happens If the Stock Price Falls Below the Strike Price of the Put?

In the event the underlying security ("underlying") is falling rapidly, the put buyer may wish to exercise her option and force the option seller to purchase her shares at the strike price on, before, or after market close of expiration.

For example, if you had sold a $500 put on TSLA and TSLA closes on expiration day at $480, then you would be "assigned" the shares at $500. That means you will have to buy her shares for $500 per share x 100 shares per contract. If you sold 5 puts at that strike and expiration, then you would be assigned 500 shares.

So why is the put seller willing to take this lopsided transaction in the put buyer's favor?

Because you must remember that not only did the put seller take in a premium which he still gets to keep, but this is a stock the put seller would not mind owning, at or below the price where it was trading when the seller sold the put. The put seller was bullish on the stock, and still is.

Put it Simply

And, perhaps most importantly for the skeptics, if the put seller had originally just purchased the long-stock back when it was travv ,mding at say, $600, instead of selling the $500, then the put seller would now be down $120 per share instead of being able to buy the shares for a $100 discount per share AND retaining the full premium.[2]

Selling Out-of-the-Money Options Gives You More Chances to Win Compared to Buying Stocks

When you are buying out-of-the-money (OTM) calls, such as one with a .20 delta strike price, you are buying a lottery ticket (albeit with more favorable odds than an actual lottery ticket) with roughly an 80% probability that your stock will not make a jump of sufficient size, within sufficient time, for the OTM call to become in-the-money (ITM).[3]

To put this into context with an actual example, let's say on 22 DEC 2020 you want to buy a .20 delta call option on SPY with an expiration about a week out. SPY is currently trading at $367 on 22 DEC 2020. Looking at the options table on your app or desktop, you would clearly see the nearest strike to the .20 delta would be $373 strike with a 30 DEC 2020 expiration. Remember that both the option buyer and option seller each choose which strike and which expiration date to buy or sell, just like a merchant chooses which items to sell and a buyer chooses which items to buy. So when your order fills, you will now have 7 calendar days for SPY to make a move towards, and above, your $373 strike. Assuming all other Greeks remain constant, for each day that SPY stays flat or goes down, you will see an unrealized loss on your call option, as time decay eats away at the value of your call each day. If SPY fails to make at least a $7 move, your call option will expire worthless and you will forfeit the $89 you spent to purchase it a week ago. The reason it needs to make at least a $7 move upward is because you will have no reason to exercise a $373 call option on SPY if SPY is trading at $373 on the open market, since you can just go out and buy it and avoid paying a potential commission and exercise fee from your broker.

And if SPY goes up to $374 the following trading day, you're still out of luck. Your call option will have expired worthless, and you will have suffered a 100% loss of the premium you paid the option seller for the right to purchase the shares at the predetermined strike price by the predetermined date.

So while buying an OTM call option at a .20 delta gives you roughly an 80% probability of losing as an option buyer, it would seem to follow that by reversing the roles, we would also be reversing the probabilities of success. In other words, rather than being an option buyer with a 20% probability of success, we could act as the option seller, and enjoy an approximate 80% probability of success by selling OTM options.

When you buy stocks, you essentially have only two ways to make a profit: 1) the stock appreciates in value, 2) the stock pays a dividend. However, dividends are rarely enough to offset losses that stocks frequently suffer, so option #1 is your primary path to success.

When you sell an OTM option, not only does the stock have to 1) make a potentially significant move, but it must 2) make that significant move in the right direction, and must do so 3) before the expiration of the option.

---

[2] There will usually be a slight commission (nowadays often lower than $4 per contract) that your broker will charge you when buying or selling options. Any mention of "full premium" or "100% of the premium" is irrespective of this commission.

[3] ITM: A put option is in-the-money if the market price is below the strike price.

Now while the focus of this eBook is on selling puts, there are several significant benefits to selling calls. I will discuss the benefits of selling OTM calls in another eBook, especially the highly successful strategy of selling OTM calls on shares you already own. This is called a covered call, and if you sell the call at a strike price at which you would be happy to exit the shares for a profit, then this too is a win-win strategy regardless of whether the strike is hit or not.

Part II: A More Detailed Explanation of the Strategy and Terms

Basics of Put Options

This eBook discusses how to use options, specifically put options, as a trading strategy. In the context of puts, a trader can either buy a put option or sell a put option. So let's quickly review what a put option is.

A put option is a contract. Whoever purchased the put has the right, *but not the obligation,* to offload 100 shares per put at a specific price ("strike price") within a defined period ("expiration period"). If the right is not exercised by the expiration period, the put expires "worthless".

There are two parties involved: a put buyer (called the **option holder**) and a put seller (**option writer**). The two parties don't contract individually. Rather, the matching of put sellers to put buyers is all handled electronically, in real-time.

The put buyer may own the shares for which they are buying the put as a hedge, or may have purchased the put without owning the underlying shares as a speculative investment.

The buyer of the put pays a premium to the put seller. This is because the buyer of the put is buying the right to sell his shares to a guaranteed buyer any time on or before the put's expiration.

The put seller should have already set aside cash in a margin account to cover the value of the shares if the option is exercised at the strike price. The brokerage facilitates the exchange, thus enforcing the put seller's obligation.

A **naked short put** is when a put is written without the cash to cover it. The put seller wants to pay less for the shares of the underlying stock should they be assigned. The put writer expects that the stock will trade above the strike price until expiration, at which time the option becomes worthless so he doesn't anticipate the need to have cash available to buy the shares because the put will not be assigned.

Common Objections By People Skeptical of Selling Naked Options

WIth naked puts, if the underlying stock's price closes below the put's strike price, the put seller must be prepared to purchase the shares at the strike price, even though the actual value of the shares will be less. Remember, the reason you are willing to accept this risk is that you wanted to own the shares at a price lower than where it was trading when you wrote the put contract.

What if the stock plummets far below the strike price? The put seller will be forced to buy a stock that is worth less than what he paid for it!

Again, we are talking about the "worst-case scenario" here. But is it really a worst-case scenario? Remember, you have already taken in a premium for selling the put. Next, by selling an OTM put, the previous owner of the shares has already suffered the drop in value from where the stock was trading when you sold the put to where the stock is trading now. So those are losses you have avoided personally.

But most objectors can never get past the final consideration:

The put seller will be forced to buy a stock that is worth less than what he paid for it!

Yes, on paper, this will look like an unrealized loss. But here's what most skeptics fail to take into account in their dismissal of selling naked puts: **The seller of the put wanted to own the shares, and took in a premium while he waited for the price to drop to a price equal to or lesser than the price at which he wanted to own the shares.**

One way to conceptualize the selling of an OTM naked put is to compare it to a buy-to-open limit order on long stock. When you route such a limit order, you are telling the broker that you would like to purchase the shares of a stock, but only at or below the limit price. Once the order is routed, the broker immediately sets aside a cash/margin amount equal to the amount required to purchase the shares at the limit price. In order for the limit order to be filled, the stock price will have to fall.

When a limit order fills, it means that the buyer is buying the shares at a discount compared to where he would have acquired them if he had routed a market order instead of a good-till-canceled limit-order. However, the buyer does not receive a premium while he waits for the limit order to fill, whereas the put seller does.

So, once the price has dropped, you will have not only retained your premium, which can partially offset the unrealized paper loss, but you have also lowered your cost basis, potentially far below the price where the stock was trading when you first sold the put and would have been willing to buy.

If you had originally just bought the shares, instead of selling an OTM put, not only would you have suffered an even greater loss, but you wouldn't have received the premium payment.

One might also object:

I wouldn't have ridden the stock down because I always use stop-losses to get me out.

If you currently use stop-loss orders, you would be wise to do some reading and researching on the studies that have likened stop-losses to "profit-losses," as the nature of high-frequency trading makes them prone to intraday swings that might have you unintentionally exiting profitable positions via "get me out at any price" market orders. So while stop-losses/stop-limits are certainly risk-reducing strategies, their advantages must be weighed against their drawbacks.

To clarify, the main reason why selling a naked OTM put on a stock you want to own is similar to owning long-stock is that in both situations, the long-stock can plummet far below a strike price, theoretically to zero, and whether you A) bought the long-stock at $100 before it went to zero, or B) were forced to buy it at $80 after it hit zero via assignment, both parties are suffering a loss, but the individual in situation A is suffering a larger loss and receives no premium (albeit potentially a small dividend).

Why Would Anybody Buy A Put Option?

Buying a put option is a way to limit the investor's losses on individual stock transactions. The put option has value only if the underlying stock is trading at *less* than the strike price at which the investor purchased the option at the time the option expires. If TSLA is trading at $800 and you purchase a $700 put option expiring in one month, the put is a guarantee that the most you can lose per share is $100. This is because you purchased the put for $700. The $700 is its strike, or exercise price. If TSLA closes anywhere *below* $700 one month from now, before your put expires, you can exercise your option as a put buyer and force the put seller to purchase your 100 shares of TSLA at the strike price of $700, even if TSLA is trading far lower than $700, such as $600, $500, or even $0, one month from now when your put option expires. If you hadn't purchased a put option, you could end up losing your entire investment in the stock.

I always learn fastest through examples, so here are two more examples.

1. TSLA is currently trading at $604 on Tuesday, Dec 1st. Buyer purchases a $575 put option expiring on Friday, December 18th. TSLA closes on Friday, December 18th at $674. In this case, the $575 put option that the buyer purchased will expire worthless. Why? Because the buyer was only buying protection in the event that TSLA closes below $575 on Friday, December 18th. Since TSLA closed far above that level ($674), the buyer of the put option will have no reason to exercise their put option and will forfeit the premium paid for the put protection because that strike price was never reached.

2. TSLA is currently trading at $604 on Tuesday, Dec 1st. Buyer purchases a $575 put option expiring on Friday, December 18th. Midway through this period, on December 9th, TSLA drops to $570. Will the buyer exercise her put option now? The answer will almost always be no, because there is still another week remaining on the option. Technically the put buyer could exercise her option anytime before the expiration date (European options don't allow this). If she exercises the option before it expires, she will receive the guaranteed price of $575 per share, which limits her loss on the investment if the market drops further than $570. However she would also have to surrender her shares to the put seller. She would be wiser to wait and see if TSLA recovers some of the decline in its value over the next week. If she holds on to her shares until the option expiration date and in the interim the market recovers to $575, she could sell her shares on the open market to limit her loss, rather than exercise her option. If the market continues to rise, the option will expire worthless and she could benefit from the increase in capital appreciation on the shares.

Risks of Short Put Selling

The put seller's main risk is that he or she is contractually obligated to buy a predetermined quantity of shares, at a predetermined strike price, within a predetermined time frame.

Under the American options system, the put buyer can exercise her option to dump her shares and force the put seller to buy the shares she is dumping at any time up to the put contract's expiration date.

Remember that the put buyer has the right, but not the obligation, to exercise her option.

So of course selling put options will be considered risky, and here's why. If you sell a put option on a stock, you are promising to purchase the stock at the strike price any time the buyer of the put option decides to exercise her "right, but not obligation" to force the put seller to purchase the shares. The main reason this is risky is that the stock price could have plummeted during the time the option was sold, forcing the seller of the put to be obligated to purchase the shares at a higher price per share than the shares' instant market value.

The put seller voluntarily accepts this risk because he understands that OTM options, especially those with a delta lower than -.60 are less, rather than more, likely to expire out of the money, thus entitling the put seller to retain 100% of the premium before commissions (which are usually less than $4 per contract nowadays).

Remember that a -.60 delta strike price roughly correlates to a 40% probability the underlying stock will make a move large enough to catch up and surpass this OTM strike by the expiration. Also remember that the majority of OTM options expire worthless for option buyers, thus an option seller is placing the same odds that routinely work against option buyers in the favor of the option seller.

Another Risk: Liquidity Lockup

It is patently obvious that when you purchase a security, your available cash or margin balance will decrease.

So when you sell a put, your broker will normally set aside enough cash or margin, via a "maintenance requirement" for you to be able to own the shares if they are "put" to you.

There is not a uniform answer as to what percentage you will be expected to set aside because it depends on the volatility of the stock and whether you have portfolio margin, standard margin, or no margin at all. But one way to get an idea of how much this will be is to look at your order confirmation page before you confirm the order. One of the figures it will show you is your resulting buying power for stock after you submit the order. That will tell you how much cash or margin balance will be set aside and how much you will have remaining after the order goes through.

Again, don't be scared away by this. When you have owned stock in the past, you had to keep cash or margin set aside in direct proportion to the stock value and number of shares.

Why Would Anybody Sell A Put Option?

Now that you have been apprised of the risks of short-put option selling, perhaps you are *still* unconvinced that the reward/risk ratio doesn't balance in your favor.

Again, as an option seller, you are promising to buy somebody's shares if they fall below a predetermined price target by a given predetermined time or expiration period. with the uncertainty that is inherent in individual stocks and the market in general, why would any prudent trader voluntarily enter a contract to purchase somebody's shares at a value below their market value at a future date?

Here are the two primary reasons why the risk of short put option selling is not only worth taking, but why it is largely less risky than the typical strategy you're probably used to of "buy, hold, hope." This is because options are based on mathematical probabilities, rather than highly speculative, and routinely unreliable, fundamental or technical analysis trading techniques. As I will mention in a subsequent section "Choosing the Strike Price," you don't need to be strong at math to understand options. The complex derivative calculations are done for you behind the scenes. Once you've decided on what stocks you'd like to own, you just need to decide at what strike and expiration to sell the short put.

Reason #1 You are selling out-of-the-money put options on stocks you are bullish on and would want to own. This means you are promising to buy the stock, but only if you can get a discount from where it's currently trading. So if TSLA's market price is currently $645 and you sell the $540 strike put expiring in about a month, you could be obligated to buy TSLA if it falls by at least $106 by the end of that expiration period. Technically you could still be exercised (forced to buy the shares) if it falls by less, or before the expiration, but either occurrence would be rare.

*Notice the increases in premium for similar strikes for each month. Selling this $545 put strike about a month from the time this screenshot was taken would yield about $1,150 in premium. Always look at the price in the "Bid" column when selling options, regardless of whether you're selling a call or a put. The "Ask" price is what you will pay when you are **buying** a call or a put.*

Reason #2 You are being compensated for your promise to buy the shares. In the above example, by promising to buy TSLA if it falls by $100 from its current market price from $645 to $540, you will be compensated with a premium of $1,150 at the current limit order bid price for the 22JAN2021 $540 put according to the options tables.

If you recognize that what I just explained is a repeat of what I discussed in the earlier chapter, it was intentional because it is crucial to hear it again.

New concepts are best absorbed when they are repeated more than once in more than one way.

I know that a strategy that incorporates naked puts will reflexively be a turn-off to many traders who fail to recognize it can actually be a less risky option than a conventional strategy of buy, hold, hope, in which you are only making money if your stock is moving up or paying a dividend. Under that conventional strategy, for every dollar your stock is going down, your loss is exactly proportional to the number of shares you own.

However, with an OTM naked put selling strategy, you will often/normally show a profit on days the underlying stock stays flat, or goes up. And as you get within the last few days before expiration, you will still be making money even on days where the underlying stock is falling, so long as your out-of-the-money (OTM) remains OTM.

How Can You Sell a Put If You Don't Already Own The Shares?

The option seller doesn't need to own the shares at the time he sells the put. The put seller only needs to own the shares when the option buyer obligates the option seller to purchase her shares.

This is because a put option provides the option buyer with the right, but not the obligation, to force the option seller to purchase the buyer's shares at a predetermined strike price.

I know the concept of the option seller "buying" the shares and the option buyer "selling" the shares will be confusing to many, so let me explain it more clearly.

When somebody buys a put option, they are normally doing one of two things:

> **Hedging** - Purchasing downside protection for the shares they own at a cost normally far less than what the actual losses per share would be if their long stock were to fall to that level.
>
> **Speculating** - Purchasing a put option as a speculative investment. This is often done by purchasing put options whose underlying price is lower than where the stock is currently trading (aka "out-of-the money") with the hope that the underlying stock will make a sizable move downwards and the put option strike price that used to be far away from where the stock's market price was currently trading is now gets close to, or higher than, the current trading price of the stock. The buyer can then exercise his option and earn a profit from the difference between the higher strike price and the lower market price of the stock. In other words, for puts, the strike price of the put must be above the market price of the shares for the put to have any value at expiration. When this happens, the put has "intrinsic value."

So what is the "buyer" of the put option actually "buying"? The put option buyer is "buying" is the right to offload her shares at a predetermined strike price in the event her stock tanks. Since nobody would be willing to buy somebody's shares at a price higher than they could purchase them on the open market, the option sellers are "selling" downside protection and must be compensated for the risk that they are willingly accepting.

To phrase it a different way: a put buyer is buying downside protection. A put seller is selling that downside protection.

And the reason the put seller doesn't need to own the put before selling the put is because by selling a put, the seller has agreed to buy the shares at a future date if and when the put buyer decides to exercise her put option.

Unless and until the put option buyer exercises this option, the put seller doesn't have the obligation to buy the shares.

Who Can Sell A Put?

In order to be eligible to sell naked puts, you will need to have a margin account and you will need to be approved for option selling, so talk to your broker. I strongly urge you to learn and hone this strategy using a virtual trading account before you start risking actual capital. There are problems with every brokerage and trading platform, but I find TDAmeritrade has the fewest, and I really like their PaperMoney and OnDemand virtual trading and backtesting tools available in TDAmeritrade's Think or Swim platform.

To be provisioned to sell ("write") options, you generally need to request permission from your broker. Some brokers will require you to submit an online request and take a quick online test to determine your proficiency to trade or sell options. This is because options can be risky. If that frightens you, then stop investing altogether right now. Can you think of a zero-risk investment in any field? If so, go put all your money there.

Most options traders find it helpful to have a margin account (very few would be able to trade in volume in a cash account).

Margin allows you to leverage your money in order to be able to buy or sell securities that you could not otherwise afford by buying only with cash. This too can be risky, as you might be doubling or tripling your spending power. Think of this as similar to buying on credit. Again, this isn't necessarily something to fear, as you probably already did this when you bought your home and/or car. So you already understand the obvious risks of buying anything on credit, namely, that you could end up owing more than your asset/liability is worth and since you don't actually own the asset, you run the risk of being unable to pay back the margin money.

If you do not have a margin account established, you must have enough cash in your cash account to be able to purchase 100 shares of the stock you are writing an option on at its current market price.

Basic Concept Summary

We have discussed many concepts so far, so let's do a comprehension check to calibrate our understanding.

>**Put Buyer.** The put buyer spends money to purchase the "right, but not the obligation" to offload her shares at a predetermined price ("strike price") on or before a predetermined "expiration date."
>
>**Put Seller.** The put seller promises to purchase a put buyer's shares at a predetermined price on or before a predetermined expiration date, in exchange for an opportunity to purchase these shares at a discount, while collecting a premium for undertaking this obligation.
>
>**Strike Price.** The price at which the option seller will be forced to purchase the underlying shares if the put option right gets exercised by the buyer.
>
>**Expiration Date.** The expiration date is the latest date on which a call or put can be exercised by the put buyer.

Put it Simply

Out-of-the-Money (OTM). If the put's strike price is lower than the stock price, then the put is out-of-the-money. Depending on how many days are remaining until expiration and how close the strike is to the stock price, the OTM put might still have "extrinsic value."

In-the-Money (ITM). If the put's strike price is higher than the stock price, the put is in-the-money. This also means that the put has "intrinsic value" and will have more value than what the put buyer paid for it.

How Often Can You Sell A Put?

Not all stocks are "optionable," meaning that not all stocks have options available to trade on them. But of the stocks that are optionable, nearly all of them have expiration dates at least once a month, generally on the third Friday of the month. Many, but not as many, have weekly expirations every Friday. And a few ETFs now have tri-weekly expirations on Mon, Wed and Fri (such as the "SPY" ETF).

A monthly expiration doesn't necessarily mean you must sell with 30 days remaining. Rather, you can decide to sell at any time before the expiration. So for a Friday, 22JAN2021 expiration, you could sell a put at any time before expiration, whether 3 months out, 1 week out, or even the morning of Friday, 22JAN2021.

You can also sell longer term puts with expiration dates one year out, and in some cases, even longer. LEAPS or **L**ong term **E**quity **A**ntici**P**ation **S**ecurities are options with expiration dates from 1-3 years.

One advantage of selling puts close to expiration is the speed at which their time value deteriorates. In other words, the time window that remains for the underlying stock to make its move before expiration will be closing rapidly as expiration draws near. It can be a relief to see a put do a mid-day reversal from loss to profitability on expiration date as the underlying stock is plummeting but not enough for the stock to cross below the put's strike price. After the close of extended-hours trading on expiration date, so long as your put expires ATM or OTM, you should see nearly a 100% profitability. In other words, so long as the put you sold expires worthless, you will keep all of the premium you sold the option for, typically minus a small commission. .

In general, the further out you sell a put before its expiration, the more premium you will collect. This is because you are increasing the length of time during which the stock can potentially make a wild move in either directionthus increasing the risk. Obviously, there would be less time for a stock to make such a move when you write ("sell"), for example, intraday options. Of course there are exceptions, such as selling immediately before earnings, but exceptions don't make the rule. The rule is that the amount of premium you will take in, all other factors (or "Greeks") being constant, is generally far greater the farther out you sell the put from its expiration date.

However, if you wait to sell a put on days in which implied volatility (IV) is high, typically on days the stock is plummeting, or immediately before earnings, you might find that the premium you collect on days like these is far greater than on days where IV is low. Occasionally, you can collect nearly the same premium selling a weekly put in a high IV environment as you can selling a monthly put in a low IV environment.

So how often can you sell a put? The answer is: as often as you'd like. Whenever I have a put option that has expired or that I bought close to expiration, I generally sell a new one ("write a new contract") as soon as the stock is down again. This approach lets me wait for the "Black Swan" events that come irregularly but inevitably, in which IV and premiums are peaking.

Why Not Sell A Call As Well?

By selling a call in addition to selling a put, you face the risk of your shares being called away from you well before expiration date due to dividend assignment risk. What this means is that an option buyer may wish to own the stock prior to the stock's ex-dividend date so that he or she will be the holder of record on the stock's record date in order to collect the dividend. This can happen even when the call is OTM.

Remember the essential difference between selling a call and selling a put. When you sell a call, you are promising to sell your shares to the call buyer at a predetermined strike price. When you are selling a put, you are promising to buy the shares from the put buyer at a predetermined strike price.

By selling a put, especially on a security that you actually want to own, you are not only giving yourself a chance to own a desired security at a lower cost basis, and taking in a premium as you do it, but you are also avoiding dividend assignment risk.

Nevertheless, selling calls has many benefits and should be studied and considered for most portfolios as another means of lowering cost basis and securing a buyer at a desired profit target for your shares.

Potentially in another book, I will talk about the strategy of selling both an OTM call and a put, an options strategy known as either a **"strangle"** or an **"iron condor."** Both "delta-neutral" strategies afford you up to twice the profitability of selling just a short put because you are selling a put and a call and making a premium on both.

Another way selling a call can be profitable is through a strategy called a "covered-call." In this strategy, you own at least 100 shares of the stock and you sell an OTM call at a strike price for which you would be happy to sell the shares for a profit. For example, if your 100 shares of TSLA are valued at $600/share, and you sold the $700 strike expiring in a month, you would take in a premium for selling the call and you would keep $100 in profit if your call gets exercised, which would force you to sell them for $700, if TSLA is trading higher than $700 by close of the expiration period. I hesitate to say that this is a "risk-free" strategy, because no strategy is. However, the risk here is not a risk of loss, but rather that you are risking capped profits because the most you can make on a covered call is the difference between the share price and the strike price, plus the premium you took in.

If I write a book on call options strategies, I will discuss the aforementioned strategies in depth. But in this book, the focus is on strategies involving only puts, as you are more likely to emerge with a working knowledge of a strategy by focusing on one strategy in some depth compared to trying to learn some things about multiple strategies and coming away with nothing but confusion about all of them.

The path to mastery comes from going deep, not wide.

Choosing the Strike Price

My profession as an attorney doesn't involve handling a lot of complicated math. I don't know who you are, but you are presumably no worse at math than I am. So don't worry about the complex calculations; these are done for you in the options tables. You just need to experiment through risk-free backtesting and paper money virtual accounts to find out which delta gives you the best balance of risk/reward.

The primary consideration in choosing a strike price is to determine whether or not you would like to eventually own the underlying shares.

- A) **Increase the likelihood of owning the shares.** If you are ready to own the shares now, then you will want to set a strike price very close to the current underlying price. The closer you set the strike, the greater the likelihood you will get assigned the shares, because the smaller the jump for the stock to make for it to finish ITM by expiration. The great thing about this is that the closer you set the strike to the underlying, the more premium you will earn. This can be a nice win-win.
- B) **Decrease the likelihood of owning the shares.** If you are primarily interested in just collecting regular premiums, then you will want to set your strike farther out. Keep in mind that you must still have the willingness and ability to own the shares, but your likelihood of owning them under this strategy will be lower. A rule of thumb might be to never sell higher than a .20 delta (technically a -.20 delta when referring to puts), so that you will hover around a 80% chance of not getting assigned. It is so easy to determine what strike price correlates to this. One way is to look at the deltas on the options table. Another way is to enable the "probability OTM" column in your options table.

Tweaks I've Discovered to Extract More Premium

Education tends to be expensive. Normally, you have to pay someone to teach you or you are going to pay by learning things the hard way.

So here are some tweaks I have learned through expensive experimentation and by frequently learning things the hard way.

1. Look at which expiration month has significantly higher IV

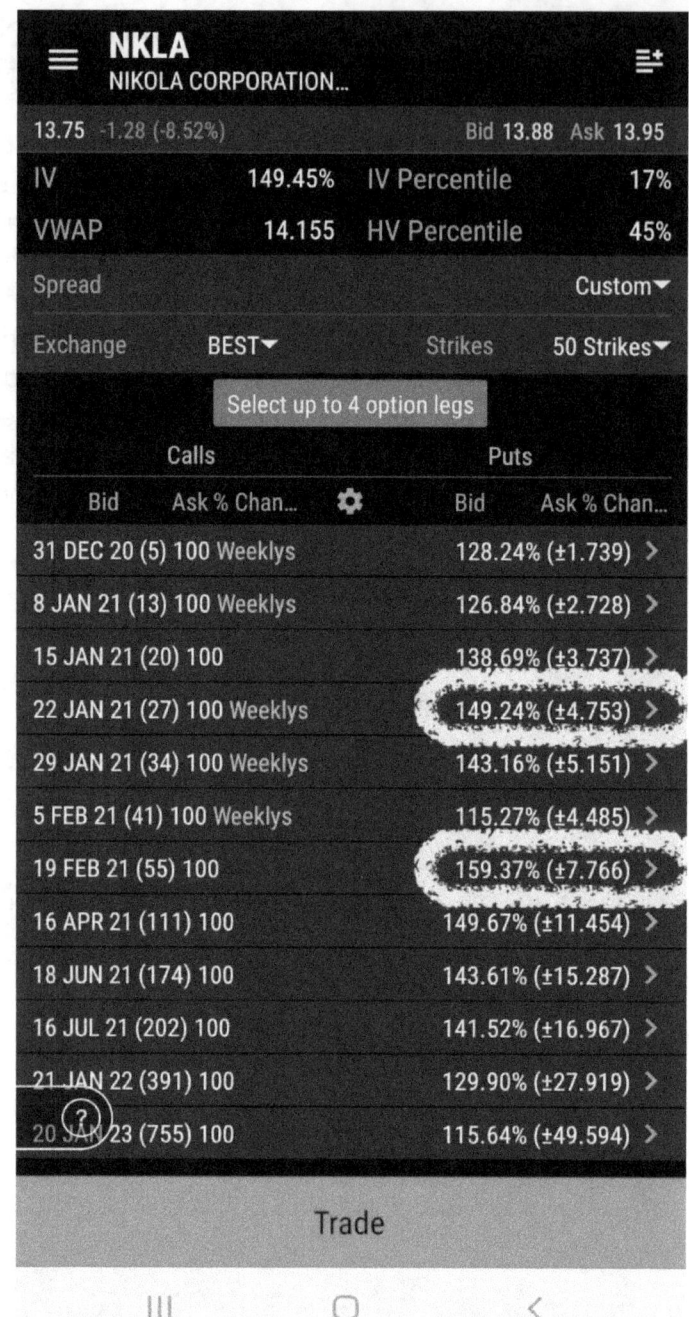

Here you can see how on 22 JAN 2021 and 19 FEB 2021 IV is spiking relative to nearby expiration dates.

2. And as mentioned earlier in this book, always wait for a day in which the stock has been trading down for at least a day. That will usually bring an automatic increase to IV. Remember, IV makes an option more valuable, which means you will get more premium for the same strike (all other factors being constant).

NKLA — NIKOLA CORPORATION...

13.75 -1.28 (-8.52%)   Bid 13.88 Ask 13.95

Calls Bid	Ask	% Chan...	Strike	Puts Bid	Ask	% Chan...
29 JAN 21 (34) 100 Weeklys					143.16%	(±5.151)
5 FEB 21 (41) 100 Weeklys					115.27%	(±4.485)
19 FEB 21 (55) 100					159.37%	(±7.766)
10.80	11.70	-16.31%	2.5	0.05	0.15	40.00%
8.50	9.40	-12.62%	5	0.15	0.20	25.00%
6.20	7.00	-10.47%	7.5	0.50	0.55	57.14%
4.50	5.10	-21.54%	10	1.05	1.10	27.06%
3.00	3.40	-23.10%	12.5	1.90	2.10	17.14%
2.05	2.20	-27.59%	15	3.30	3.60	20.34%
1.35	1.50	-26.70%	17.5	5.10	5.40	19.32%
0.80	1.00	-31.11%	20	7.10	7.60	18.70%
0.55	0.70	-27.17%	22.5	9.30	9.70	10.51%
0.40	0.55	-41.25%	25	11.60	12.10	9.11%

Trade

Here you can see how on a day in which Nikola is down the put premiums are spiking showing a positive "% change" for each put strike price. Notice that the $2.5 strike put is showing a 40% increase in the premium available.

3. Lastly, you will sometimes see that the bid price between two puts is very close, perhaps just a matter of a few pennies. Remember, the farther the strike price is OTM, the more likely it will expire OTM and thus entitle you to 100% of the premium (minus commission). So if you can sacrifice a dollar or less in profit to get a strike that's more than a dollar lower, go for it. In other words, if I take in $100 in premium for selling the $50 strike put, or $99 in premium for selling the $45 strike put, why not go for the lower delta $45 strike put? This way you are lowering the strike price of your OTM by an additional $5 to ensure that the option goes OTM in exchange for giving up just $1 in profit.

Here you will see that you will sacrifice about $150 in premium if you opt to sell the $535 strike instead of the $545 strike. You will also see that the differential between the strikes is the smallest for the jump between the $535 and $537.5 strikes compared to the other sets.

Put it Simply

If You Don't Want to Own the Stock Immediately

If you don't want to own the stock because something about its attractiveness has changed, there are 3 strategies you can use:

1. You can buy back the put option at a higher price than when you sold it. The magnitude of your unrealized loss from the purchase of the put options will be partially offset by the premiums you earned selling put options.
2. You can buy a put at a lower strike price than your naked put. For example, you sell a put at $400 and then buy another put at $300, so the most you could lose is the differential between the two strike prices.
3. You can roll out the option to a later expiration date. In this case, you think the stock is just suffering a temporary setback but has bullish potential in the future. You will buy a put option to close out your current short position and then will sell another put option with a later expiration date. This essentially gives you more time for the stock to reverse its decline and give you a longer opportunity to be correct.

When You're Losing By Selling A Put

The main risk in selling puts is that they will end up being exercised, which can happen in a highly volatile market, or with a stock that is subject to large price swings. The put seller will acquire the underlying shares, but if several put options are exercised simultaneously or in close succession, the put seller needs to have enough cash available in his account to cover each position he wrote a put contract for. The more puts written, the larger the margin or cash reserve required. Otherwise the broker could liquidate other assets in the brokerage account to provide the cash needed to purchase the shares if the options are exercised by the option buyer. The amount of premium earned on each contract will not compensate for the money spent to buy the shares if the put buyer exercises her options.

What happens if the stock's trading price is rapidly falling towards the strike price and the put seller decides he doesn't want to own the shares after all? Maybe he has changed his mind about the long term prospects of the stock because of negative news.

In this case, the put seller can close out his obligation to purchase the shares, by buying the option he has sold back from the buyer, which he can do anytime before expiration. This is called **buying to close** because the put seller is closing the position he opened when he wrote the original put contract. Basically, the put seller buys back the option from the buyer. He has to give the put buyer the market value of the option, which has now increased in value because the shares have a lower trading price and the option has become more valuable to the put buyer. The option seller loses money in this transaction because the price that the put option is worth is now higher than the price when the put seller originally sold the put.

What Happens If the Stock Price Doesn't Fall to the Price of your Put?

When selling OTM puts, the ideal occurrence is that the option expires worthless and the put seller keeps the premium even though he or she doesn't acquire the shares. The put seller has the opportunity to keep writing new puts as each option expires, until the share price falls to a price at which the option is eventually exercised, at which time, the put seller can acquire the shares they wanted at a lower cost basis, all the while collecting premiums from the puts that they wrote. The following examples illustrate this concept:

1. Stock X, which you would like to own, is trading on Dec 1st at $100 and you write a contract (100 shares) for a put with a 1-month expiration and a strike price of $80. At the end of the month, the stock is trading at $95. The premium for the put is $6 per share. The put expires worthless at the end of the month but you have earned $600 in premium on the contract.
2. On January 1st, you write a second monthly contract for $80 and at expiration, the stock price is $90. You still don't have the shares, but you have earned another $600 in premium.
3. On February 1st, you write a 3rd contract and this time, by its expiration at the end of February, the stock price has fallen to $80 per share. The option holder exercises their option, for which they have paid $600 in premium. As the put seller, you end up buying 100 shares of Stock X at $80/share for a total cash outlay of $8000. You have also earned a premium of $600 per contract x 3 contracts = $1800. Your overall cost for the shares is $8000-$1800= $6200. Had you bought the shares long on Dec 1st, you would have paid $10,000 for them instead.

Case Study: March 2020

Just about anyone who sold puts on any of the T-FAANG equities (TSLA, FACEBOOK, APPLE, AMAZON, NETFLIX, GOOGLE) during the second half of the month in March 2020 on each day the markets tanked could have done well. This is because indices such as the S&P 500 made a literal V-shaped recovery on March 23rd, 2020.

If you were assigned the long shares of those equities back in March, you would have been long just in time for one of the greatest V-shaped recoveries in recent history. Just look at the prices on any of those T-FAANG stocks from March 2020 to the rest of 2020.

If you weren't assigned the shares, then the premiums you took in during March would have been enormous, as IV was figuratively exploding upwards and peaked for the S&P 500 on 16 MAR 2020. Remember that IV is a risk premium, which is like an added layer of value for a put option. So the 17 APR 2020 put sold in February 2020 would have been far less valuable than the put option sold during the turbulence of March 2020.

Exceptional months like March 2020, and even just a handful of truly exceptional days each year, are why you should always have cash on hand ready to invest.

But keep in mind, situations like these only come rarely (that's why they're known as "Black Swan events"). But when they do:

> **It takes a rare combination of insight, resilience, tenacity and fortitude to stay on the plunging airplane as everyone else is jumping off, knowing that you just need to hold out a little bit longer until the plane soars again, this time to even greater heights.**

Oftentimes, those who jump off are experienced passengers who have been on smoking planes in the past which did not soar to new heights, but instead plowed right into the ground, so their prior experience has conditioned them to expect an adverse outcome again.

Put it Simply

When Should You Take Your Profit?

The put seller can buy back the put to close out their position in the stock anytime before expiration. As the put seller, if your goal is consistent profits, it's a good idea to have a specific profitability target, at which you are willing to close out your position by buying back the option early, rather than waiting until it expires.

For example, assume you have sold one put with a $70 strike price two weeks ago with a premium of $3 per share. You will receive $300 in premium (minus commission) if your put expires worthless.

Instead of waiting for this put to expire, you can buy the same put back for cheaper than you sold it. Normally, OTM puts can be purchased back at a discount because, all other Greeks being equal, time will have degraded the value of the option.

So if the value of the $70 strike put was $3 two weeks ago, and the put strike is still lower than the market price of the stock, that means the put is OTM and the put strike might be worth $1 now. Thus, you could buy back the $70 strike before expiration for a $200 profit.

When market volatility decreases, that also might be a good time to buy back put options. Remember, the greater the volatility of the market, the higher the premiums on put options.

If on the other hand, the put seller wants to own the shares and is looking for a lower cost basis, he or she would not close out their position but wait till the option expires in the hope that the stock will close lower than the strike price of the short put. The option seller is not disappointed, because he now owns the shares at a lower price than he would have in the open market. And as consideration for waiting, he was also rewarded with a nice premium.

CONCLUSION

This eBook should have given you a basic understanding of put options and how they can be used as part of a comprehensive strategy by traders who are either looking to earn income or to expand their stock portfolio with securities purchased at a discounted cost basis.

If you found this book helpful to you, it would be helpful to me if you could leave a positive review. If you would like to hear about other strategies I employ, such as the "covered call," which allow you to regularly lower the cost-basis on securities you already own, please mention this in your review.

www.ingramcontent.com/pod-product-compliance
Lightning Source LLC
Chambersburg PA
CBHW080821220526
45466CB00011BB/3649